Whose Eyes Are These?

ELIZABETH BURMAN PATTERSON

Tommy
NELSON

Thomas Nelson, Inc.
Nashville

ACKNOWLEDGEMENTS

A loving thank you to
Matthew Parkes
&
Sheppard and Jim Franz
for their generous help with
the thoughtful, happy poems.

And to
David G. Patterson
for his
encouragement and love.

DEDICATED TO

My grandchildren
Nathan and Anna
and all the children in the world
May they love and protect
All God's Creatures

LIBRARY OF CONGRESS CATALOGING-IN-PUBLICATION DATA

Patterson, Elizabeth Burman.
  Whose Eyes Are These?/watercolors by Elizabeth Burman Patterson
  p. cm.—
  Summary: A collection of poems in which various animals describe themselves,
their physical attributes, and their behavior.
  ISBN 0-8499-1464-7
1. Children's poetry, American. [1. Animals—poetry.
2. American poetry.] I. Title
  PS3566.A818W48 1997
  811'.54—dc21
                                                              97-6790
                                                              CIP
                                                              AC

Printed in the United States of America
97 98 99 00 RRD 9 8 7 6 5 4 3 2 1

INTRODUCTION

YOU ARE ABOUT TO HAVE A WONDERFUL ADVENTURE. You are going on a sight seeing safari. What's a safari? It is a trip you go on to see animals. You are going to get to see them in a very special way. You'll get up close, very close and look them right in their eyes. Isn't that exciting?

I know the artist who painted all these pictures. You can find her name right on the cover of this book. I can tell you she likes you. How do I know? Because she made a beautiful book for you. She smiles and talks to people in loving ways. She is smiling at you and telling you she loves you.

REV. BERN BRUNSTING

Minister Emeritus,
Christ Church of Quaker Hill
January 17, 1997

I am curious by nature,
I climb with my claws.
A ball of soft yarn,
I can push with my paws.

Whose eyes are these?

cat

I have long floppy ears,
and a tiny pink nose.
I'm fuzzy and furry,
Right down to my toes.

Whose eyes are these?

rabbit

I look like a horse,
I'm black and I'm white.
You may think I'm odd,
but God made me just right.

Whose eyes are these?

zebra

I am king of the beasts,
in Africa I roam.
When my family's together,
Our pride is our home.

Whose eyes are these?

lion

With long hairy arms,
I swing through the trees.
I eat lots of fruit,
and sleep where I please.

Whose eyes are these?

orangutan

My home is the forest,
I live in the trees.
I run and I climb,
and eat bamboo leaves.

Whose eyes are these?

panda

Come to Australia:
look up in the trees.
I'm there with my mates,
chewing Euchalyptus leaves.

Whose eyes are these?

koala

My memory is long,
and so is my nose.
Everyone calls it a trunk,
but it hangs to my toes.

Whose eyes are these?

elephant

You may hear me say *Whooo,*
and think I am wise.
I can see well at night,
with my great big eyes.

Whose eyes are these?

owl

God looked down at me,
"What a jumper you'll be."
So I hop and I splash
and in the water I dash.

Whose eyes are these?

frog

I creep through the jungle
searching for prey.
Then rest in the long grass
in the heat of the day.

Whose eyes are these?

tiger

With a bushy ringed tail,
and a mask on my face,
I live in a hollow tree,
It's my favorite place.

Whose eyes are these?

racoon

I run and I bark,
and I play with my toys.
I am man's best friend,
but I love girls and boys.

Whose eyes are these?

Bop

These eyes are my eyes,
they allow me to see,
God made me so special,
there's no one like me.

Whose eyes are these?

mine